LOVE, LOSS, AND WHAT I WORE

Written and illustrated by

ILENE BECKERMAN

Algonquin Books of Chapel Hill 2005

Published by
Algonquin Books of Chapel Hill
Post Office Box 2225
Chapel Hill, North Carolina 27515-2225

a division of Workman Publishing
708 Broadway
New York, NY 10003

First paperback edition, Algonquin Books of Chapel Hill, April 2005.
Originally published by Algonquin Books of Chapel Hill in 1995.
Printed in Mexico.
Published simultaneously in Canada by Thomas Allen & Son Limited.

Design by Robbin Gourley.

Library of Congress Cataloging-in-Publication Data

Beckerman, Ilene, 1935–
    Love, loss, and what I wore / by Ilene Beckerman.
      p. cm.
    ISBN 1-56512-111-2 (hardcover)
    1. Costume—New York (N.Y.)—History—20th century.
2. Beckerman, Ilene, 1935–   . 3. New York (N.Y.)—
Biography. I. Title.

  GT617.N4B43   1995   95-20460
  391'.009747'10904—dc20   CIP

    ISBN 1-56512-475-8 (paper)

10 9 8 7 6 5 4 3 2 1
First Paperback Edition

To the wonderful women in my life

my mother,
my grandmother,
my aunt Babbie,
Miriam Landey,
Dora and Gay,
Bonnie,
Isabelle, Lillie, and Julie,
Allie, Olivia, and Chloe,
and Elisabeth

The   1 9 4 0 s

My Brownie uniform.

My mother was a Brownie leader at Hunter College Elementary School, 69th Street, between Lexington and Park.

When I was seven, I went to Camp Brady, a sleep-away camp in Brewster, New York, for Brownies and Girl Scouts. My sister, who was five years older, was a Girl Scout and looked after me at camp.

There was no electricity. We had no flush toilets and had to go in an outhouse.

A store-bought brown dressy coat with matching leggings (to keep legs warm) and galoshes (to keep feet dry). I hated putting on the leggings (which were held up by suspenders) and always had a tantrum.

Note the brightly colored mittens. My mother was an excellent knitter and was always making mittens for my sister and me. My sister inherited her knitting skill and made argyle socks, using many bobbins.

Rag curls were a popular hairdo.

You made them by tearing old sheets and pillowcases into strips (white was the only color they came in), wrapping the strips around dampened hair, and tying a bow at the bottom.

After a night's sleep, the rags would be carefully undone and beautiful long curls would appear.

While my mother made our curls, we'd listen to our favorite radio programs. My favorite was *The Lux Radio Theater* because they acted out movies on it.

We lived at 333 East 66th Street, between First and Second Avenues, in a first-floor railroad flat that faced the front. One room was connected to the next in a straight line, like railroad cars.

My mother made this gray-and-white-striped seersucker pinafore with red rickrack trim.

She made almost all of my sister's and my clothes and we had many "sister" dresses. This was one of my mother's favorite patterns. She also made it in a floral chintz with lace trim.

My sister wore a blouse under her pinafore. I didn't have to.

I wore this black taffeta outfit to dancing school at
Ballet Arts in the Carnegie Hall building on 57th
Street.

Note colored embroidery across the midriff. My mother
made this for me. I liked it very much, but what I really
wanted was a store-bought outfit.

Sometimes I would take the crosstown bus to Ballet
Arts by myself. My mother would walk me to the bus.
She would yell at me for wearing perfume and mascara
but forgetting to wash my neck.

My mother made this plaid taffeta party dress for my tenth birthday. Note the unusual neckline—straight across—and tiny black velvet bows on each shoulder.

The dress made a wonderful swishing noise when I walked. I wore it to school the day of my birthday and got a lot of attention.

When I walked, I "turned in" on my heels so I had to wear special shoes with arch supports from a store called Julius Grossman's. Everybody else wore loafers or saddle shoes and for parties red or black Mary Janes, but my shoes were brown and had laces. For parties, I had a brown pair with buckles on the side.

White dickey with Peter Pan collar, wool sweater, plaid wool-wrap pleated skirt with safety pin, and high white knee socks.

A typical outfit I wore to elementary school.

My mother made this black velvet hat, lined in quilted red satin. It had decorative trimming and tied under the chin. Sonja Henie, who was an ice-skating movie star, used to wear similar hats.

It used to be very important to keep your ears covered and warm so you didn't get an ear infection.

Everybody said I looked good in hats. This other hat is a "scotty" hat my mother bought for me. I wore hats on Easter Sunday and Passover.

My mother made this pink, green, and black iridescent-metallic plaid taffeta gown. We bought the material at Macy's at Herald Square. They had a whole floor just for selling patterns and fabrics.

I wore it to my cousin Sally's wedding. We weren't friendly with that side of the family—my father's—but I was excited to wear an evening gown.

I wore a big pink bow in my hair.

Easter Sunday outfit. Coral wool suit with pleated skirt. White short-sleeved sharkskin blouse with drawstring neck.

We always got a new Easter outfit. Easter Sunday, we'd find a bench in front of Central Park, at around 65th Street, and watch the people walk up and down Fifth Avenue in their holiday outfits.

A variety of braided hairdos: Loops. Crown. "Hamburgers" over the ears.

We wore short, full jackets in springtime, which we called "toppers."

This was one I had in coral.

A new fabric was introduced called "tubular jersey" and my mother made matching dresses for my sister and me.

She crocheted a black wool border around the neck and sleeves.

My mother made this forest-green wool jersey dress embroidered with red cherries for my sister.

My sister was tall and had a voluptuous figure. Her name was Blossom, but everyone called her "Tootsie" except my grandfather. He called her "the pig" and he called me "the monkey." Everybody else called me "Gingy" because I was born with ginger-colored hair. We called my grandfather "Pop."

Later, when Tootsie married Shel, Shel didn't like her names and called her "Bonnie."

My sister had long, red fingernails and loved Frank Sinatra. She cut out pictures of "Frankie" from movie magazines (*Photoplay, Silver Screen, Screen Gems*) and taped them to the walls of the bedroom we shared. Whenever we had a fight, I would try to tear the pictures off the walls and she would scratch my arms with her nails.

I bit my nails and they were very ugly.

My mother made this sexy red dress for my sister. It had a keyhole neckline and peplum and was accented with hand-sewn gold sequins.

Peplums were very popular in those days.

Sewing on the sequins was tedious work. My mother also sewed multicolored sequins on printed silk scarfs, which we'd give to our teachers for Christmas. Sometimes we gave them fancy soap or flowered handkerchiefs instead.

Black faille dress with a shocking-pink silk rose at the waist.

This was one of the few dresses my mother didn't make. She bought it for my sister on sale at Henri Bendel's on West 57th Street.

My sister wore it when Shel came back from the army before they got engaged.

She bought another black dress when Shel was wooing her. Note illusion sweetheart neckline.

My mother made this gorgeous green taffeta strapless gown for my sister to wear to our cousin's wedding.

Note silk flowers (sewn on elastic band) worn around upper arms. The skirt was extravagantly full.

My mother was a large, handsome woman who didn't wear fancy clothes, maybe because we couldn't afford them. Once my grandmother surprised her with a silver fox stole (for her birthday or Mother's Day, I can't remember which). My mother tried it on but never wore it after that day.

She usually wore a dark print dress and brown shoes with a buckle. For a while she worked as a nurse's aide and would wear a blue-gray jumper over a white blouse. But she never had the kind of cape the nurses had in paper-doll books.

Even though she was a Brownie leader, she never got a Brownie leader's uniform. It was too expensive.

She had a premature white streak in the front of her hair. She never wore make-up, only sometimes a little lipstick that she would put on without looking in the mirror and then make even by pressing her lips together.

She wore glasses. Her face had a beautiful shape and her eyes were hazel.

The spring after my mother died, my father took me to B. Altman's department store on Fifth Avenue to buy a dress for my thirteenth birthday.

I selected two navy-blue dresses (see this page and next). This one had a removable cape collar. Each dress was very expensive, about forty-four dollars.

I wore one of them to the thirteenth birthday party I had with my friend Jean Lowrie. Her birthday is June 10. Mine is June 15.

Jean's mother took us to the Stockholm Restaurant for a birthday lunch with some of our school friends. My grandmother gave her money for my share.

One day my grandmother came and got my sister and me. She didn't want us to live with my father but with her and Pop and my aunt Babbie.

They owned a brownstone building at 743 Madison Avenue, between 65th and 66th Streets, and had a stationery store on the street level. It was called Harry Goldberg's. They lived above the store.

After we went to live with my grandparents, I never saw my father again.

Jean, who lived at 24 Central Park South, picked me up at the store every morning and we'd walk together to Hunter College Junior High School at 68th and Lexington Avenue.

My grandmother's name was Lillie but we called her Ettie. She had very beautiful, long silver-gray hair that she twisted up on top of her head into a bun that she called a *draidel*, keeping loose waves in front.

She used two large haircombs to keep up the hair in back and several large hairpins to keep the *draidel* in place.

She put Vaseline on her hair to keep it nice. She believed in two cures: Vaseline for anything wrong outside the body and hot tea with lemon for anything wrong inside the body.

My grandmother usually wore a navy-blue or charcoal-gray cardigan sweater in the store, no matter what the weather was.

The sweater had two large pockets into which she would slip quarters from the cash register.

She told us that she was saving the quarters for me and my sister but we never got them.

The telephone number of the store was RHinelander 4–8096.

My grandmother, like many older ladies, rolled her stockings below the knee instead of wearing garters.

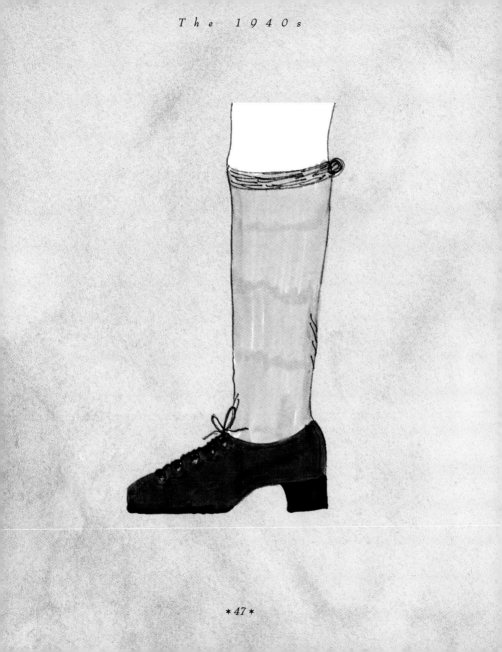

I wore this black bathing suit when I went to Florida with my grandmother. I was fourteen.

I met a boy on the beach named Bernie Maybrook from Allentown, Pennsylvania. He was twenty-six. He wanted to go on a date with me, and my grandmother said okay as long as she could go, too. So she did, along with Bernie's father.

The 1950s

I bought this cotton waffle-weave dress in
Bloomingdale's basement. It was red and black and had
a Mexican look to the print.

I went with my friend Judy Gellert to buy it. Judy went
to Hunter College High School with me. She lived
downtown in Stuyvesant Town.

I had another friend at Hunter named Marilyn
Herman. She had long blond hair and was pretty but
fat. She wore her clothes too tight. Her mother also
had long blond hair and wore big "picture" hats. She
was also very pretty and fat and she worked in a court.
Nobody else's mother worked. Marilyn had no father.

I wore this blue lace dress with white collar and blue satin cummerbund when I was confirmed at Temple Emanu-El, 65th Street and Fifth Avenue, on May 18, 1951. I was sixteen. The rabbis were Dr. Perlman and Dr. Marks.

Everyone in my confirmation class had a topic to speak on. We didn't choose the topic; it was given to us. Mine was "Mercy."

My hair was short and I had bleached it blond with a bottle of peroxide. Whenever my friend Dora saw a woman with a terrible bleach job, she would always say, "Almost as bad as you, Gingy."

My sister wore a green dress with vivid cerise flowers, and a hat with flowers.

After the ceremony, my grandmother made a small party for me at the Alrae Hotel on 64th Street, around the corner from the store.

My aunt Babbie (her real name was Pauline) had enormous breasts. She never got married.

She had very beautiful small hands. Once someone asked her if she wanted to be a hand model but nothing ever came of it.

She had her nails manicured every Saturday afternoon with Revlon's Windsor pink nail polish. She also had her eyebrows arched and her hair done.

After the beauty parlor, she would take my sister and me to lunch, usually at Child's Restaurant, and then to a movie—preferably a double feature at Loew's 72nd Street or RKO 58th Street.

On one of her hands she wore a black onyx ring. On the other, a marquise-shaped ring with diamonds and emeralds, which I wear now.

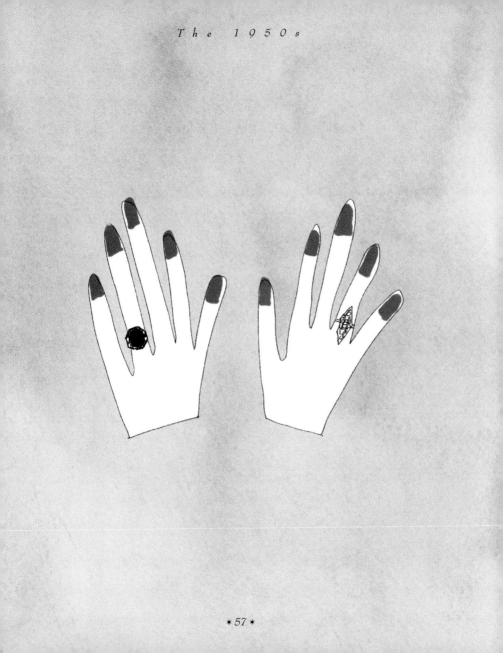

In high school, my friend Fran Todtfeld and I would go to an Army-Navy store to buy real sailor middy blouses. We also bought pea jackets there.

My friend Gay and I wanted to have "basketball sweaters" but we had no team and no boyfriends to give us their sweaters.

We found a store on the Lower East Side that made those sweaters to order but you had to get at least four. So we found two more girls who wanted sweaters and formed a club. We chose maroon sweaters with white stripes and white writing.

You were supposed to have the name of your team on the back of the sweater, but since we had no team, we had no name. We decided on WC'WD, which stood for "We Couldn't Think of a Name, So We Didn't."

When we went to order the sweaters, the salesman measured our chests with a tape measure. We thought he was very vulgar.

Once we had the sweaters, we gave up the club.

A typical outfit worn to high school (Riverdale Country Day School) by my best friend, Dora.

Long-sleeved, white silky blouse with pearl buttons, black ballerina-length full skirt, and black ballet slippers.

Dora usually wore her long, straight, shiny black hair in a high ponytail.

Note Dora's real beauty mark at the end of her eyebrow.

Dora lived at 22 East 65th Street, across from my grandparents' store.

Color looked gorgeous on Gay, my second-best friend. She usually wore a chiffon scarf—pink, turquoise, aqua, lavender, or purple—knotted around her neck, and a purple sweater.

The color of the scarf and sweater brought out the extraordinary colors in her eyes, eyelids, and cheeks. She said she never wore eye-makeup but I didn't believe her.

Gay and I made these yellow-and-black-striped cotton circle skirts. It took forever to hem them.

Gay lived at 30 East 70th Street. Gay and Dora were my best friends. They still are.

Gay had a brother named Peter. He was three years older, taller, darker, and kept to himself.

Gay's parents were Armenian. Her mother's name was Zabelle. She made yogurt, wore white satin nightgowns, and read lots of books. They had a baby grand piano in the living room that she played. She visited friends who weren't feeling well. She used to tell Gay to speak more softly and to speak through the front of her mouth.

Gay's father's name was Zarah. He was very handsome and an architect. He also painted Utrillo-like scenes in oils. He drank martinis and often went out with beautiful women. When I went to their house in the morning, sometimes he'd be sleeping on the couch in the living room. I never said a word to him nor he to me.

Long-sleeved black turtleneck jersey, gray quilted circle skirt (or gray accordian-pleated skirt when I could borrow it from Dora), and wide leather belt from Greenwich Village.

This is how we dressed when we went out on a "plain" date to someplace like Jimmy Ryan's to hear Dixieland or to the movies.

We got more dressed up when we went to the Rainbow Room on top of the RCA Building, the Persian Room at the Plaza, or the Columbia Room on the Astor roof.

My grandmother bought me this dress from MacWise, a very exclusive store between 65th and 66th Streets on Madison. The people who owned the dress store were customers in my grandparents' store, so my grandmother got it for very little when they couldn't sell it.

The dress was much too sophisticated for a high-school girl, but my grandmother didn't know that. It was strapless, with rows of black velvet alternating with rows of black faille. It was very tight.

I wore it to a party I went to with Dora on the West Side. We usually didn't go to the West Side because we lived on the East Side and we were snobby. We thought the boys on the West Side were too fast. I almost got into trouble at that party (very rare because I was so shy). I think it was because of the dress.

Another dress from MacWise. Although the neckline was much too low, I loved this black-and-brown-striped dress and often wore it on dates.

This red T-strap was a favorite "going-out" shoe. Dora and I wore them but Gay's feet were too big to wear that style.

Most of the time we wore black Capezio ballet slippers, which we bought on the sixth floor of Bonwit Teller's on Saturday afternoons.

I bought this coat at Klein's on 14th Street. It had very avant-garde styling—like a sweater. Dora's mother saw it and told Dora to get one, too. Mine was red and green. Dora's was purple and blue.

Dora's mother, Miriam Landey, was a dress designer for rich ladies who lived on the West Side. She would go to Europe in the summer to buy fine and fancy fabrics. She designed only a few styles but made them up in different fabrics.

Her showroom took the entire second floor of 22 East 65th Street. Dora and her parents lived on the third floor. Seamstresses, who did exquisite beading, worked in the back room on the second floor, surrounded by mannequins padded with tissue paper to duplicate the full figures of customers.

Dora's mother always hired beautiful models to show the clothes. The models changed behind a mirrored screen with cupids on it. Dora's mother loved cupids.

Dora's father's name was Harry. He drank martinis and listened to WQXR.

Perfume

Tigress

White Shoulders

Belodgia

We bought our make-up at Liggett's Drug Store on the corner of 65th and Madison. We'd sit at the counter and order grilled-cheese sandwiches and cherry cokes while we talked about what color nail polish to buy.

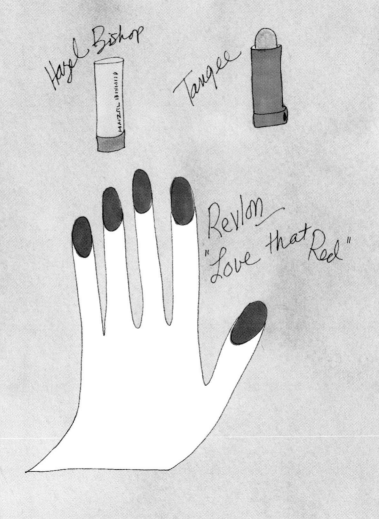

Typical underwear we wore on a date: girdle, garter belt, and stockings with seams. If we had our periods, we also wore a sanitary belt and a Kotex or Modess pad. We wore underpants over everything, then a half-slip, then a crinoline.

Crinoline petticoat worn under skirts and dresses to make them stand out. Often we wore several crinolines.

If you forgot to wear a half-slip, the crinolines would frequently make runs in your stockings.

Dora's mother lent me this gown when Dora and I went to the Choate School for Boys in Connecticut for the weekend. The dress was mauve satin with delicate beadwork on the bodice. It had a long train.

We carried our evening dresses (we each took up two evening dresses) in a huge black-zippered dress bag.

Dora had a real date for the weekend with a boy named Lee. We used to laugh at him because he thought he was very good looking (we didn't) and his clothes smelled from mothballs. He was very, very rich.

Dora fixed me up with a blind date. Whenever Dora went someplace special, her mother would say, "Take Gingy along." So Dora had arranged for the blind date.

We took the train from Grand Central to Choate. It was full of other girls also going for the weekend. They were very preppy and gave us mean looks.

My blind date was named Jim. I didn't like him. I met another boy, also named Jim, and liked him. We necked a lot.

My evening dresses were much too sophisticated for Choate. Some of the preppy girls called us whores. Probably because of the dresses and the necking.

The Jim I liked wrote me love letters for several months after the weekend. I got embarrassed when I read them.

This was the other evening dress I took to Choate— black taffeta. I remember also wearing it to the Horace Mann senior prom. I went with a boy named Larry Janos. After the prom, we went to the Copacabana on 60th Street off Fifth Avenue, double-dating with Larry's best friend, David, and his girlfriend.

Dean Martin and Jerry Lewis were the attraction. We sat ringside, drank Tom Collinses, and smoked Pall Malls. I stole a Copacabana ashtray.

For another prom I had a teal-blue ankle-length ballerina dress with a full tulle skirt worn with several crinolines. I don't remember the boy I went with or the prom, just the dress.

Babbie had a beautiful ice-green flapper dress with silver beads from when she was young. She kept it in her drawer. I wore it to a costume party at Dora's and the silver beads kept falling off.

In another drawer, she kept a long, thick, auburn braid that my mother had saved from when she was young and had cut her hair. It was about fourteen inches in length, and I sometimes wore it as a chignon.

For my Hunter College High School senior
photograph in the 1953 yearbook, I wore a white
dotted-swiss blouse with large, bouffant sleeves.

I wore it backwards because I thought the neck looked
more attractive on me that way.

This is the coral wool jersey dress I bought for a New Year's Eve date with George Feifer, in 1954. I was madly in love with George.

I saw it in the window of a store on 58th Street and Lexington Avenue and admired its boat neck and princess styling.

I had planned to go "all the way" with George that night but it didn't happen.

We went to a party in Passaic, New Jersey. My friend Marion Brody—we both went to Simmons College in Boston—came too. I got her a date with a friend of George's.

I thought after we drove Marion home we would have a wonderful opportunity to "do it." But we had car trouble and George was driving. He had to drop me off first.

Light-blue ensemble—coat, cashmere sweater, and matching skirt I wore to the Harvard/Dartmouth football game.

George and I had broken up and I was going to the game with a blind date. I borrowed this outfit from a friend in my dorm.

I selected the outfit very carefully because I thought wearing all light blue would make me stand out (most of the girls wore very bright colors, especially red) and George would see me.

Light-blue bridesmaid dress I wore to Gay's wedding to Steve Chinlund. Steve was very handsome. He looked like a combination of Mayor Lindsay and Charlton Heston.

Dora was also a bridesmaid.

We felt daring because we weren't wearing our bras under the dresses (the square neckline was too low) and no one ever went without a bra back then.

The wedding was gorgeous but not as gorgeous as Gay and Steve.

Pink satin princess-style dress I bought in Filene's Basement in Boston for my marriage to Harry M. Johnson in 1955. I was twenty and Harry was thirty-seven.

Harry was my sociology professor at Simmons and had a Ph.D. from Harvard. He also taught at the Massachusetts School of Art. His income from both positions was $5,000 a year.

Harry's mother's name was Helen. Harry was 6'4" and his mother was almost as tall. She had been widowed when she was young and worked in security at Harvard, and, when she got older as an attendant in a ladies' room at Harvard. I liked her very much.

Harry and I were married at his best friend's house in Dobbs Ferry. His friend's name was Bernard Barber. He taught sociology at Barnard and had married a very rich girl. Robert Merton, the Columbia sociologist, was best man. There was no food, only champagne and wedding cake.

My grandmother and Babbie came to the wedding. My grandfather wouldn't come because he thought Harry was too old for me and because he was Catholic.

I wore this yellow dress after the wedding ceremony on our drive back to Cambridge. The dress was one I had bought at MacWise. I later dyed it red. We drove up Route 1 to Boston in Harry's light-blue Dodge. We had our wedding dinner in a truckstop.

Our first apartment was at 888 Massachusetts Avenue in Cambridge. Later we moved to 27 Lanark Road in Brookline.

Black dress with cut-out neckline and matching bolero jacket.

Harry always liked me to wear my hair off my face.

I could wear very high heels with Harry because he was so tall.

I never called Harry by his name. I called him "Man."

Iridescent-brocade Chinese-style dinner dress I bought in Cambridge for a New Year's Eve party that Harry and I went to on the eve of 1957.

Harry went with me to buy a dress. He convinced me to buy this one even though it was expensive. He said it showed off my arms, which he thought were pretty. I loved the dress.

The party was at the home of Harry's friends Penny and Ecky, in Wayland, Massachusetts. I got very upset because I couldn't find Harry at midnight. Then I saw him kissing Penny.

After my divorce, I went back to New York and lived with Dora, who was studying to be an actress.

This yellow-ochre wool empire dress was Dora's but I wore it a lot. I particularly remember wearing it on a date with Al Beckerman.

Floral-print cotton pique dress I purchased in a small, snooty store in New Canaan, Connecticut, for my marriage to Al.

The ceremony took place in the rabbi's chambers in Rego Park, Queens.

The reception was held in Al's parents' house in Forest Hills.

I used to call Al "Becky."

My grandmother and Babbie came to the wedding. My grandfather wouldn't come. He was still mad at me for marrying Harry.

Al's father, Jack Beckerman, gave me this two-piece gray organza Anne Fogarty dress. It had a beautiful accordian-pleated skirt. Anne Fogarty was a very popular, expensive designer but since Jack was a pattern-maker in the garment industry, he was able to get it wholesale.

I accidentally burnt a cigarette hole in it.

I think one of my daughters has the dress now.

The 1960s

Black-and-red-print taffeta maternity dress worn to holiday parties.

First worn Christmas, 1960, in Stamford, Connecticut, when I was pregnant with Isabelle, and then in 1962 when I was pregnant with David. (David died when he was eighteen months old from a forty-eight-hour intestinal virus.)

Also worn after we moved to Livingston, New Jersey, when I was pregnant with Lillie in 1963, Michael in 1964, Joe in 1965, and, for the last time, when I was pregnant with Julie in 1967.

I was influenced by Audrey Hepburn and Jackie
Kennedy when I bought this white empire dress at
Loehmann's in Florham Park, New Jersey. I hadn't
bought a dress in a long time. I only went to the food
store or the pediatrician. I shouldn't have bought the
dress because by then my body was nothing like Audrey
Hepburn's or Jackie's.

I wore the dress to Al's Christmas party at the
advertising agency where he worked. I had rushed to get
the children settled, to pick up the baby sitter, and to
catch the Lakeland bus to New York—so I didn't eat. I
was so hungry when I got there, I ate too many hors
d'oeuvres and drank too much champagne too quickly. I
threw up in the ladies' room. Though none of it got on
my white dress, I never wore the dress again.

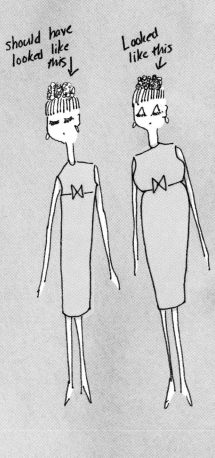

should have
looked like
this ↓

Looked
like this
↓

The 1970s, 1980s,

and 1990s

Copy of a Pucci minidress I bought on impulse at Bloomingdale's. I was never comfortable wearing it. I thought it was too bright and too short and that I would run into somebody else wearing it who looked a lot better in it than I did. My therapist told me I shouldn't feel guilty if I didn't want to wear it.

I wore Al's ties occasionally because I'd seen pictures of Marlene Dietrich, Greta Garbo, and Katharine Hepburn wearing ties, but when the movie *Annie Hall* came out and everybody started wearing men's ties, I stopped wearing them.

My grandmother let me have my ears pierced when I was thirteen. She went to the doctor with me to have it done. Julie, my youngest daughter, came home from the mall one day with three holes in each ear when she was twelve. I told her I thought it was barbaric to have so many holes, but the following year I went to the mall and had a second hole made in my left ear.

I ordered this beige wool pants suit from the Spiegel catalog. It was my first mail-order purchase. I thought it would be a good interview outfit because, now that the children were all in school, I wanted to get a part-time job.

When I was offered a job as a public relations assistant, I accepted. According to the women's magazines, having a job qualified me to be one of those lucky women who had it all—a husband, children, and a career. But things hadn't been the same between Al and me since the baby died.

I loved this print jersey Diane Von Furstenberg wrap
dress. It was easy to put on and very comfortable. I
wore it the day I had my hair cut and permed at
Sassoon's in New York.

Driving home, I knew I had to tell Al that I couldn't
stay married to him anymore.

I bought this three-quarter-length long-haired raccoon jacket from Bonwit Teller's fur department in the Short Hills Mall. I had opened a charge account in my own name after I got a job and it took me a year to pay for the jacket. I was glad I had bought it, though, because after Al and I separated, money became tight.

Getting ready to sell the house, I went through the attic and basement and made three piles of clothes—those to throw out, those to give away, and those I didn't know what to do with but couldn't throw out or give away.

For my fiftieth birthday, I had the bags removed from under my eyes and bought these black suede boots on 8th Street in the Village. I recalled that Al's mother had been fifty when I first met her. She'd never owned a pair of high heels in the sixty-five years she'd lived. When I think of her, I always picture her with a dish towel over her shoulder.

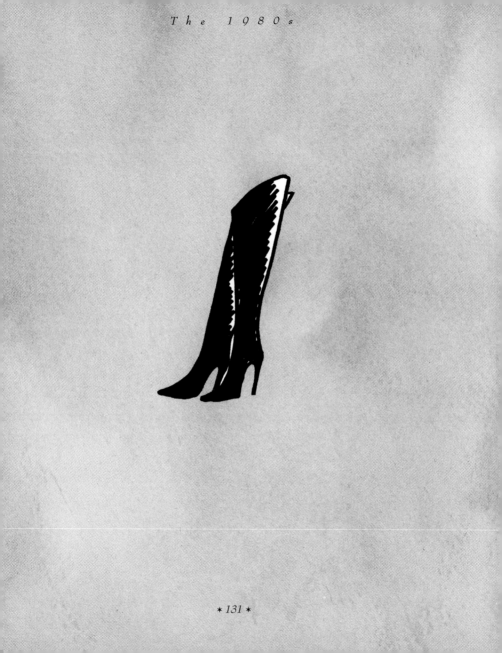

For Isabelle's wedding, I wore a short white silk pyramid dress with white embroidery on the collar and cuffs that I had bought at a Neiman Marcus outlet store. By the time Lillie got married a year later, I felt more confident. I wore a black strapless faille dress that reminded me of one Rita Hayworth wore in the movie *Gilda*. Over it I wore a Donna Karan long white silk shirt.

When my first granddaughter, Allie, was born, I found some of my daughter's baby things in one of the boxes I had saved and gave them to the new baby.

Now that Allie's four, she loves to play dress-up when she comes over. I polish her fingernails and toenails bright red and let her play in the drawer where I keep all the awful colors of lipstick, rouge, and eyeshadow that aggressive saleswomen talked me into buying.

But what Allie really loves are my boxes of old clothes, high-heels, and hats. I watch her face as she looks in the mirror and sees how beautiful she looks in my old dresses. I wonder if she'll remember some of them when she gets older.

Recently I spoke to Dora. We call each other once or twice a year. I asked her if she ever thought about the clothes we wore when we were growing up.

"Never," she said. "It was such a painful time."

I keep thinking about what she said. I always thought she'd had a fairytale life—a mother, a father, beautiful clothes, and even a beauty mark.

E P I L O G U E

Sometimes if I can't sleep at night I think about how my life used to be when I was young.

Some nights I try to remember my mother. I don't have too many memories of her. I can remember more things about Dora's mother. Our mothers were very different— Dora's mother wore real jewelry, sailed to Europe on the *Ile de France,* and went to the theater. My mother didn't do any of those things.

But they also had things in common. Both made clothes (Dora's mother for fancy ladies, my mother for my sister and me), and both died when they were young—my mother at forty-four and Dora's mother at fifty-two.

I like to think I got my fashion sense from my mother and from Dora's mother.